David Brainerd's Personal Testimony

D0728258

David Brainerd's Personal Testimony

Selected from his Journal and Diary
by Walter Searle
Foreword by Andrew Murray

BAKER BOOK HOUSE
Grand Rapids, Michigan

Paperback edition issued 1978
by Baker Book House
ISBN: 0-8010-8159-9

Printed in the United States of America

Second printing, February 1979
Third printing, June 1980

Foreword

GOD has no more precious gift to give to a church or an age than a man who lives as the embodiment of His will, and inspires those around him with the faith of what grace can do. We speak of the nineteenth century as one of missionary revival. It is remarkable how, in the previous century, God gave His church two men, whose biographies not only testify to intense life-sacrificing devotion to mission work, but specially help those who followed them to believe in the power of prayer as the essential element of service in the kingdom. David Brainerd and Henry Martyn were both powerful witnesses to faith in God's promise and the confident assurance that prayer would hasten the coming of the kingdom. Many a missionary who came after them owed the deepening of his faith in prayer to their example.

This little volume of extracts from the life of David Brainerd has been prepared to bring some of the passages having reference to his intense and powerful praying within reach of all Christians. The one thing one could wish to say to all readers is: Beware of being content, and even delighted, with what you read of the intensity of Brainerd's prayers, and the wonderful answer that sometimes came so speedily and with such power. This delight may tempt you to rest content with the approval and the pleasure of knowing what he did. But this will profit little. Read, and pause, and read again, as in God's presence, until you hear the voice of the Spirit calling you to follow in the footsteps of God's servants. Ask grace to enable you to prove what the secret is of such intense love to souls, and such confident assurance that God will, in answer to your prayer, too, bestow blessing on those for whom you pray.

And let us pray very specially that the church may be convinced of the sin of prayerlessness, and of the blessed possibilities of a life crying day and night to Him for His blessing on those who are still in darkness.

May God bless every reader of the book.

ANDREW MURRAY

Contents

Few but Blessed Years

FOR many years past while living among the heathen in South Africa, I have constantly used Brainerd's example as an incentive to wrestling in prayer and the unflagging pursuit of holiness; and frequently I have referred to his diary and journal when speaking at missionary meetings during my time of furlough in England. This reference has often raised the question, Who was Brainerd?, showing a lamentable, if not considerable, lack of knowledge of this "prince with God and men"; and inquiry has followed as to where his book can be obtained.

It is hoped that this condensed selection from his immortal pages will supply an oft-expressed need and want, and the lines emphasized will call attention to those remarkable expressions which have struck us in our private reading of the pages which glow with fire divine

David Brainerd, whose passion for prayer glows in these following pages, was born in America, April 20, 1718, of godly parents. Awakened by God's Spirit in boyhood, he found salvation when about twenty years old. He attended for the next three years Yale College, from which he was most unrighteously expelled for one unguarded expression, the outcome, not of malice against his professor, but of youthful zeal for genuine religion. His diary breathes only a spirit of benevolence and forgiveness towards those who had sorely injured him.

He began to preach at the age of twenty-four, and labored among the Indians of New Jersey and Pennsylvania from 1743 to 1747. A brief but marvelous ministry! He closed his earthly career in the house of the celebrated President Jonathan Edwards, to whose daughter Brainerd was engaged to be married.

It was most fitting that his life story should be written and his journal and diary edited by this sympathetic and devoted friend, and for the last one hundred and fifty years the book has been a source of blessing and a stimulus to the whole church of Christ.

Henry Martyn, brilliant senior wrangler of Cambridge University, was influenced by it to go forth to the heathen, forsaking all, and saying, "Now to burn out for God"—as Brainerd had already written in his diary, "I longed to be a flame of fire continually glowing in the divine service and building up Christ's kingdom to my last and dying breath."

William Carey, the "Apostle to India," not only caught for himself the holy contagion, but, in giving instructions to his coworkers, urged them continually to think of Brainerd wrestling in prayer among the solitudes of the backwoods of America.

Dr. A. J. Gordon, missionary enthusiast and advocate, declares how his torch was kindled at the altar of Brainerd's unquenchable devotion. He describes his visit to the graveyard of Northampton, and how, having found the sacred spot where one hundred and fifty years ago the bodily remains of this seraphic soul were deposited, he brushed aside the snow from the simple slab, and meditated on the far-reaching effects of a life so brief and so obscure.

It was through his prayer-passion that Brainerd wrought miracles of conversion in spite of the Indians' prejudice against him, and his own ignorance of their language; for, after eight days' prayer in the woods, he came forth endued with power, and though he preached through a drunken interpreter the Holy Spirit was so poured out that numbers were converted.

The journal has only to be read to see what kind of converts they were. Previously old, ignorant, savage, superstitious, thievish, and murderous, they brought forth works meet for repentance. They became truly holy, being suddenly illuminated supernaturally, and were so fashioned after the type of the primitive and Pentecostal Christians that the cautious Presbyterian Brainerd followed the apostolic custom of an almost immediate baptism. This singular and unusual circumstance appears in the journal, for within two months of their first hearing of the gospel, these heathen were judged faithful like Lydia, and ready to be baptized.

One other instance of the perennial effect of this record of God's dealings with and through this polished instrument of His grace is seen in the ministry of the venerable Dr. Andrew Murray of South Africa, for he, like thousands more, acknowledges what inspiration has come to him by reading the journal. In a recent letter to me, Dr. Murray exclaims, "How such examples rebuke the prayerlessness and lukewarmness of most Christian lives." And it is his suggestion that a small volume like this should be issued to arouse missionary fervor and a passion for prayer, especially among the friends of missions—contributors, local helpers, committees, councils, and missionary study classes, that they may pray as real spiritual warriors in God's prayer legion.

In his study at Wellington, South Africa, looking out on the purple mountains, he once said to me: "You will find three pages of the diary are sufficient to read at one time if you desire to be influenced by it immediately and practically." This I have found to be the case.

I have kept a little book of extracts on my study table near my Bible, and I have never laid it down without the determination at once to pray and wrestle fervently for the heathen, even as Brainerd prayed. I therefore issue it with confidence that, if it is read slowly and prayerfully, its immediate effect will be to lead to the practice of prayer. Other elaborate treatises may lead to discussion of the philosophy and problems of prayer, but our Lord says: "Enter thou into thy chamber, and pray to thy Father in secret."

The value of this little volume will be that it will bring us into living touch with one who actually embodied in his conduct three great Christian graces: (1) A sublime passion for God's glory; (2) A persistent pursuit of the loftiest holiness; (3) A daily practice of fervent intercessory prayer.

Space does not permit of so many quotations as we should have liked to give, illustrating how intense and habitual was this supreme passion for God's glory—such as this: "Oh, that I could spend every moment of my life to God's glory"; or this, a few days before he died: "It refreshed my soul to think of former things, of desires to glorify God, and of the pleasures of living to Him."

This was his dedication of himself to missionary toils, after having weighed in the balance a life of comparative comfort in a civilized pastorate: "Here am I,

Lord, send me to the rough, savage pagans of the wilderness; send me from all that is called comfort even to death itself, if it be in Thy service and to promote Thy kingdom.''

Surely he could say, "For me to live is Christ, and to die is gain.'' That his desire for holiness was a persistent and persevering pursuit appears on almost every page. It became, "This one thing I do.''

At the opening of his diary he dares to write, "I know I long for God and conformity to His will, in inward purity and holiness, ten thousand times more than for anything here below.'' At another time he bursts out, "Oh, that my soul were holy as He is holy! Oh, that it were pure even as Christ is pure.''

We might cite a thousand similar passages, to show how unceasing and all-absorbing was his quest, but his progress was more like the mathematical asymptote, a line which, though continually approaching some curve, never meets it; because he seems to be possessed by the traditional delusion that he must be under the fatal necessity of sinning. One could almost have wished there had been some Aquila and Priscilla to have shown him the way of the Lord more perfectly, and that while holiness is, in a sense, progressive, yet it is as instantaneous as justification, and, like it, also by faith.

One cannot but believe that if he had applied more to the all-cleansing blood, of which so little is said in his diary, we should not have had those bitter upbraidings and bemoanings of corruption, nor those awful melancholy complaints which at length he came to regard as "sinful dejection," and which hindered his usefulness.

But apart from this, his passion for God, his yearning for holiness, as well as his habitual practice of prayer, must ever make him a constraining influence. It is to this latter grace of his that our attention is specially called. Let it be carefully noted how frequently he retired for prayer, how protracted, how fervent it was, even to profuse sweat, like John Fletcher; and how this was mixed, like the prayers of Moses, Daniel, Paul, and the Savior even, with fasting. Note again how he continually says, "God enabled me to wrestle for multitudes of immortal souls."

I shall have laboured in vain if, in issuing this brief condensation of a copious and wondrous record of the holy prayerful life of him who was like the voice of one crying in the wilderness, it does not arouse ministers, missionaries, and brave helpers to pray exceedingly for the benighted heathen.

WALTER SEARLE

1
The Praying Student

We commence our selection of extracts from David Brainerd's famous journal and diary by turning to the part begun by him in April, 1742, while pursuing his theological studies under the private tuition of a godly minister, when he was only about twenty-four years of age.

April 1, 1742

I seem to be declining with respect to my life and warmth in divine things. Oh, that God would humble me deeply in the dust before Him.

Then follow several intense exclamations and longings after God, such as:

Oh, that my soul were wrapt up in divine love, and my longings and desires after God increased. Oh, my blessed God, let me climb up near to Him, and love and long and plead and wrestle and reach and stretch after Him, and for deliverance from the body of sin and death.

April 6

I walked out this morning to the same place where I was last night. I began to find it sweet to pray; and could think of undergoing the greatest sufferings in the cause of Christ, with pleasure; and found myself willing, if God should so order it, to suffer banishment from my native land, among the heathen, that I might do something for their salvation, in distresses and deaths of any kind. Then God gave me to wrestle earnestly for others, for the kingdom of Christ in the world, and for dear Christian friends. I felt weaned from the world, and from my own reputation amongst men, willing to be despised, and to be a gazing stock for the world to behold.

Lord's Day, April 11

In the morning felt little life, excepting that my heart was drawn out in thankfulness to God for His amazing grace. After public worship, God gave me special assistance in prayer. I wrestled with my dear Lord, and intercession was made a delightful employment to me.

April 15

My desires apparently centered in God; and I found a sensible attraction of soul after Him sundry times today.

I know that I long for God, and conformity to His will, in inward purity and holiness, ten thousand times more than for anything here below.

Lord's Day, April 18

I retired early this morning into the woods for prayer; had the assistance of God's Spirit, and faith in exercise; and was enabled to plead with fervency for the advancement of Christ's kingdom in the world, and to intercede for dear, absent friends. At noon, God enabled me to wrestle with Him, and to feel, as I trust, the power of divine love, in prayer. At night I saw myself infinitely indebted to God, and had a view of my failure in duty.

April 19

I set apart this day for fasting and prayer to God for His grace; especially to prepare me for the work of the ministry; to give me divine aid and direction, in my preparations for that great work; and in His own time to send me into His harvest. Accordingly, in the morning, I endeavored to plead for the divine presence for the day, and not without some life. In the forenoon, I felt the power of intercession for precious, immortal souls; for the advancement of the kingdom of my dear Lord and Savior in the world; and, withal, a most sweet resignation, and even consolation and joy, in the thought of suffering hardships, distresses, and even death itself, in the promotion of it; and had peculiar enlargement in pleading for the enlightening and conversion of the poor heathen.

In the afternoon, God was with me of a truth. Oh, it was blessed company indeed! God enabled me so to agonize in prayer, that I was quite wet with perspiration, though in the shade, and the cool wind. My soul was drawn out very much from the world, for multitudes of souls. I think I had more enlargement for sinners, than for the children of God, though I felt as if I could spend my life in cries for both.

I enjoyed great sweetness in communion with my dear Savior. I think I never in my life felt such an entire weanedness from this world and so much resigned to God in everything. Oh, that I may al-

ways live to and upon my blessed God!
Amen, Amen.

April 20

This day I am twenty-four years of
age. Oh, how much mercy have I
received in the past! The Lord help me
to live more for His glory for time to
come. I hardly ever so longed to live to
God, and to be altogether devoted to
Him. I wanted to wear out my life in
His service and for His glory.

Lord's Day, April 25

This morning I spent about two hours
in secret duties, and was enabled, more
than ordinarily, to agonize for immortal
souls. Though it was early in the morning, and the sun scarcely shined at all,
yet my body was quite wet with sweat. I
felt much pressed now, as frequently of
late, to plead for the meekness and
calmness of the Lamb of God in my
soul; and through divine goodness, felt
much of it this morning.

Oh, it is a sweet disposition, heartily
to forgive all injuries done us; to wish
our greatest enemies as well as we do
our own souls! Blessed Jesus, may I be
daily more and more conformed to
Thee! At night, I was exceedingly
melted with divine love.

April 26

Oh, my soul exceedingly longs for that blessed state of perfection, of deliverance from all sin. Oh, that I could spend every moment of my life to God's glory.

April 27

I retired pretty early for secret devotions; and in prayer God was pleased to pour such ineffable comforts into my soul, that I could do nothing for some time but say over and over: "O my sweet Savior! O my sweet Savior! Whom have I in heaven but Thee? And there is none upon earth that I desire beside Thee." If I had had a thousand lives, my soul would gladly have laid them all down at once to have been with Christ.

My soul never enjoyed so much of heaven before; it was the most refined and most spiritual season of communion with God I ever yet felt. I never felt so great a degree of resignation in my life.

April 28

I withdrew to my usual place of retirement, in great peace and tranquillity, spent about two hours in secret duties, and felt much as I did yesterday morning, only weaker, and more overcome. I seemed to depend wholly on my dear Lord; wholly weaned from all other dependences.

I knew not what to say to my God but could only lean on His bosom, as it were, and breathe out my desires after a perfect conformity to Him in all things. Thirsting desires, and insatiable longings possessed my soul, after perfect holiness. God was so precious to my soul, that the world, with all its enjoyments, was infinitely vile. I had no more value for the favor of men, than for pebbles. The Lord was my all, and that He overruled all greatly delighted me.

I think that my faith and dependence on God scarce ever rose so high. I saw Him such a fountain of goodness, that it seemed impossible I should distrust Him again, or be in any way anxious about anything that should happen to me. I now enjoyed great sweetness in praying for absent friends, and for the enlargement of Christ's kingdom in the world.

May 1

I was enabled to cry to God with fervency for ministerial qualifications, that He would appear for the advancement of His own kingdom, and that He would bring in the heathen. Had much assistance in my studies. This has been a profitable week to me; I have enjoyed many communications of the blessed Spirit in my soul.

June 12

Spent much time in prayer this morning, and enjoyed much sweetness. Felt insatiable longings after God much of the day. I wondered how poor souls live, that have no God. The world, with all its enjoyments, quite vanished. I see myself very helpless; but I have a blessed God to go to. I longed exceedingly to be dissolved, and to be with Christ, to behold His glory. Oh, my weak, weary soul longs to arrive at my Father's house!

June 14

Felt somewhat of the sweetness of communion with God, and the constraining force of His love; how admirably it captivates the soul, and makes all the desires and affections to center in God!

I set apart this day for secret fasting and prayer, to entreat God to direct and bless me with regard to the great work which I have in view, of preaching the gospel—and that the Lord would return to me, and show me the light of His countenance. Had little life and power in the forenoon. Near the middle of the afternoon, God enabled me to wrestle ardently in intercession for my friends. But just at night the Lord visited me marvelously in prayer. I think my soul never was in such an agony before. I felt no restraint; for the treasures of divine grace were opened to me. I wrestled for absent friends, for the ingathering of souls, for multitudes of poor souls, and for many that I thought were the children of God, personally, in many distant places.

I was in such an agony from sun half-an-hour high, till near dark, that I was all over wet with sweat: but yet it seemed to me that I had wasted away the day, and had done nothing. Oh, my dear Savior did sweat blood for poor souls. I longed for more compassion towards them. Felt still in a sweet frame, under a sense of divine love and grace; and went to bed in such a frame, with my heart set on God.

June 15
Had the most ardent longings after God, which I ever felt in my life. At noon, in my secret retirement, I could

do nothing but tell my dear Lord, in a sweet calm, that He knew I desired nothing but Himself, nothing but holiness; that *He* had given me these desires, and He *only* could give me the thing desired. I never seemed to be so unhinged from myself, and to be so wholly devoted to God. My heart was swallowed up in God most of the day.

In the evening I had such a view of the soul being as it were enlarged, to contain more holiness, that it seemed ready to separate from my body. I then wrestled in an agony for divine blessings; had my heart drawn out in prayer for some Christian friends, beyond what I ever had before. I feel differently now from what I ever did under any enjoyments before; more engaged to live to God for ever, and less pleased with my own frames.

August 23

Had a sweet season in secret prayer: the Lord drew near to my soul, and filled me with peace and divine consolation. Oh, my soul tasted the sweetness of the upper world; and was drawn out in prayer for the world, that it might come home to Christ! Had much comfort in the thoughts and hopes of the ingathering of the heathen; was greatly assisted in intercession for Christian friends.

August 30

Felt somewhat comfortably in the morning; conversed sweetly with some friends; was in a serious composed frame; and prayed at a certain house with some degree of sweetness. Afterwards, at another house, prayed privately with a dear Christian friend or two; and, I think I scarce ever launched so far into the eternal world as then. I got so far out on the broad ocean, that my soul with joy triumphed over all the evils on the shores of mortality.

I think that time, and all its gay amusements and cruel disappointments, never appeared so inconsiderable to me before. I was in a sweet frame; I saw myself nothing, and my soul reached after God with intense desire. Oh, I saw what I owed to God, in such a manner, as I scarce ever did! I knew that I had never lived a moment to Him as I should do; indeed, it appeared to me, that I had never done anything in Christianity; my soul longed with a vehement desire to live to God. In the evening, sang and prayed with a number of

Christians; felt the powers of the world to come in my soul, in prayer. Afterwards prayed again privately, with a dear Christian or two, and found the presence of God; was somewhat humbled in my secret retirement: felt my ingratitude, because I was not wholly swallowed up in God.

October 19

This morning, and last night, I felt a sweet longing in my soul after holiness. My soul seemed so to reach and stretch towards the mark of perfect sanctity, that it was ready to break with longings.

(These intense longings after sanctification are soon followed by confessions of failure and defeat that seem to discourage the reader and bring doubt as to the superabounding grace of God over all sin.)

The fourth part of the diary opens with this sad complaint:

November 26

Had still a sense of my great vileness and endeavored as much as I could to keep alone. Oh, what a nothing, what dust and ashes am I!

However, there presently shines a gleam of brightness on his dejected soul:

Lord's Day, December 12

I preached with some sweetness on Matthew 6:33. There was much affection in the assembly. This has been a sweet Sabbath to me, and, blessed be God, I have reason to think that my religion is becoming more refined and spiritual by means of my late inward conflicts.

(This temporary relief was shortly succeeded by such fresh gloom and temptation that in unworthiness he shrank from ever going to the heathen, although he had been designated and prepared for this high calling, and was now being sent forth by the Council.

On his way to the Indians he was so greatly cast down that, as Jonathan Edwards says, on the last day of his journey "his mind was overwhelmed with an exceeding gloominess and melancholy.")

2
First Days Among the Indians

We now reach the part of his journal which records his actual arrival among the Indians.

April 1, 1743

I rode to Kaunaumeek, nearly twenty miles from Stockbridge, where the Indians live with whom I am concerned, and there lodged on a little heap of straw. I was greatly exercised with inward trials and distresses all day, and I seemed to have no God to go to.

April 7

Appeared altogether unequal to my work. It seemed to me that I should never do any service, or have any success among the Indians.

Lord's Day, April 10

Rose early in the morning, and walked out and spent a considerable time in the woods, in prayer and meditation. Preached to the Indians, both forenoon and afternoon. They behaved soberly in general: two or three in particular appeared under some religious concern, with whom I discoursed privately; and one told me, that "her heart had *cried*, ever since she had heard me preach first."

April 20

Set apart this day for fasting and prayer, to bow my soul before God for the bestowment of divine grace; especially that all my spiritual afflictions, and inward distresses, might be sanctified to my soul. And endeavored also to remember the goodness of God to me the year past, this day being my birthday. Having obtained help of God, I have hitherto lived, and am now arrived at the age of twenty-five years. My soul was pained to think of my barrenness and deadness; that I have lived so little to the glory of the eternal God. I spent the day in the woods alone, and there poured out my complaint to God. Oh, that God would enable me to live to His glory for the future!

April 30

The presence of God is what I want. I live in the most lonely melancholy desert, about eighteen miles from Albany; for it was not thought best that I should go to Delaware River. I board

with a poor Scotchman; his wife can
talk scarce any English.

My diet consists mostly of hasty pud-
ding, boiled corn, and bread baked in
the ashes, and sometimes a little meat
and butter. My lodging is a little heap of
straw, laid upon some boards, a little
way from the ground; for it is a log
room, without any floor, that I lodge in.
My work is exceedingly hard and dif-
ficult; I travel on foot a mile and a half,
the worst of ways, almost daily, and
back again; for I live so far from my
Indians. I have not seen an English per-
son in this month. These, and many
other circumstances, equally uncom-
fortable, attend me.

As to my success here, I cannot say
much as yet. The Indians seem
generally kind and well disposed
towards me, are mostly very attentive
to my instructions, and seem willing to
be taught further. Two or three, I hope,
are under some convictions; but there
seems to be little of the special working
of the divine Spirit among them yet,
which gives me many a heart-sinking
hour. Sometimes I hope that God has
abundant blessings in store for them and

me; but at other times I am overwhelmed with distress.

May 18

My circumstances are such that I have no comfort of any kind, but what I have in God. I have no fellow-Christian to whom I may unbosom myself, or lay open my spiritual sorrows; with whom I may take sweet counsel in conversation about heavenly things, and join in social prayer. The Indians have no land to live on but what the Dutch lay claim to; and these threaten to drive them off. They have no regard to the souls of the poor Indians; and by what I can learn, they hate me because I came to preach to them.

August 15

Spent most of the day in labor, to procure something to keep my horse on in the winter. Enjoyed not much sweetness in the morning; was very weak in body through the day; and thought that this frail body would soon drop into the dust; and had some very realizing apprehensions of a speedy entrance into another world.

In this weak state of body, I was not a little distressed for want of suitable food. I am forced to go or send ten or fifteen miles for all the bread I eat; and sometimes it is moldy and sour before I eat it, if I get any considerable quantity. And then again I have none for some days together, for want of an opportunity to send for it, and cannot find my horse in the woods to go myself; and this was my case today; but through divine goodness I had some Indian meal, of which I made little cakes, and fried them.

Yet I felt contented with my circumstances, and sweetly resigned to God. In prayer I enjoyed great freedom; and blessed God as much for my present circumstances, as if I had been a king; and thought that I found a disposition to be contented in any circumstances. *Blessed be God!*

Lord's Day, August 28

Was much perplexed with some irreligious Dutchmen. All their discourse turned upon the things of the world; which was no small exercise to my mind. O what a hell it would be to spend an eternity with such men! Well might David say: "I beheld the transgressors, and was grieved." But adored be God, heaven is a place into which no unclean thing enters. O I long for the holiness of that world! Lord prepare me for it!

September 19

In the afternoon, rode to Bethlehem, and there preached. Had some measure of assistance, both in prayer and preaching. I felt serious, kind, and tender towards all mankind, and longed that holiness might flourish more on earth.

September 20

Had thoughts of going forward on my return to my Indians; but towards night was taken with a hard pain in my teeth, and shivering cold; and could not possibly recover a comfortable degree of warmth the whole night following. I continued very full of pain all night; and in the morning had a very hard fever, and pains almost over my whole body.

I had a sense of the divine goodness in appointing this to be the place of my sickness, among my friends, who were very kind to me. I should probably have perished, if I had first got home to my own house in the wilderness, where I have none to converse with but the poor, rude, ignorant Indians. Here, I saw, was mercy in the midst of affliction. I continued thus, mostly confined to my bed, till Friday night; very full of pain most of the time; but through divine goodness, not afraid of death. Then the extreme folly of those appeared to me, who put off their turning to God till a sick bed. Surely this is not a time to prepare for eternity. On Friday evening my pains went off somewhat suddenly. I was exceedingly weak, and almost fainted; but was very comfortable the night following. These words of Psalm 118:17: "I shall not die, but live," etc., I frequently revolved in my mind: and thought we were to prize the continuation of life, only on this account, that we may "show forth God's goodness and grace."

Lord's Day, October 23

In the morning I had a little dawn of comfort arising from hopes of seeing glorious days in the church of God; and was enabled to pray for such a glorious day, with some strength and courage of hope. In the forenoon, treated on the glories of heaven: in the afternoon, on the miseries of hell, and the danger of going there.

November 3

Spent this day in secret fasting and

prayer, from morning till night. Early in the morning, I had some small degree of assistance in prayer. Afterwards, read the story of Elijah the prophet—I Kings, chapters 17, 18, and 19, and also II Kings, chapters 2 and 4. My soul then cried with Elisha: "Where is the Lord God of Elijah?" Oh, I longed for more faith! My soul breathed after God, and pleaded with Him, that a double portion of that Spirit which was given to Elijah might rest on me. And that which was divinely refreshing and strengthening to my soul, was, that I saw God to be the same that He was in the days of Elijah.

Was enabled to wrestle with God by prayer, in a more affectionate, fervent, humble, intense, and importunate manner, than I have for many months past. Nothing seemed too hard for God to perform; nothing too great for me to hope for from Him. I had for many months entirely lost all hopes of being made instrumental of doing any special service for God in the world; it has appeared entirely impossible that one so vile should be thus employed for God. But at this time God was pleased to revive this hope.

My soul was ardent in prayer; was

enabled to wrestle ardently for myself, for Christian friends, and for the church of God. And felt more desire to see the power of God in the conversion of souls than I have done for a long season. Blessed be God for this season of fasting and prayer! May His goodness always abide with me, and draw my soul to Him!

November 10

Spent this day in fasting and prayer alone. In the morning, was very dull and lifeless, melancholy and discouraged. But after some time, while reading II Kings 19, my soul was moved and affected; especially reading verse 14, and onward. I saw there was no other way for the afflicted children of God to take, but to go to God with all their sorrows. Hezekiah, in his great distress, went and spread his complaint before the Lord. I was then enabled to see the mighty power of God, and my extreme need of that power; and to cry to Him affectionately and ardently for His power and grace to be exercised towards me.

November 29

Began to study the Indian tongue. Was perplexed for want of more retirement. I love to live alone in my own little cottage, where I can spend much time in prayer.

(The next day he pursued his study of the language though weak in body. A footnote by his biographer shows that this study necessitated his frequent riding twenty-four miles backward and forward through uninhabited woods, and exposed him often to extreme hardship in the winter.)

December 1
Both morning and evening, I enjoyed some intenseness of soul in prayer, and longed for the enlargement of Christ's kingdom in the world. My soul seems of late to wait on God for His blessing on the church. Oh, that religion might powerfully revive!

December 22
Spent this day alone in fasting and prayer, and reading in God's Word the exercises and deliverances of His children. Had, I trust, some exercise of faith, and realizing apprehension of divine power, grace, and holiness; and, also, of the unchangeableness of God, that He is the same as when He delivered

His saints of old out of great tribulation. My soul was sundry times in prayer enlarged for God's church and people. "Oh that Zion might become the joy of the whole earth!" It is better to wait upon God with patience, than to put confidence in anything in this lower world. "My soul, wait thou on the Lord"; for "from Him comes thy salvation."

December 29

Spent the day mainly in conversing with friends; yet enjoyed little satisfaction, because I could find but few disposed to converse of divine and heavenly things. Alas, what are the things of this world, to afford satisfaction to the soul!

Near night, returned to Stockbridge. In secret, I blessed God for retirement, and that I am not always exposed to the company and conversation of the world. Oh, that I could live "in the secret of God's presence!"

December 31

Rode from Stockbridge home to my house. The air was clear and calm, but as cold as ever I felt it, or nearly so. I was in great danger of perishing by the extremity of the season. Was enabled to meditate much on the road.

Lord's Day, January 1, 1744

Of a truth God has been kind and gracious to me, though He has caused me to pass through many sorrows. He has provided for me bountifully, so that I have been enabled, in about fifteen months past, to bestow to charitable uses about a hundred pounds, New England money, that I can now remember. Blessed be the Lord, who has so far used me as His steward, to distribute a portion of His goods. May I always remember, that all I have comes from God. Blessed be the Lord, who has carried me through all. Oh, that I could begin this year with God, and spend the whole of it to His glory, either in life or death!

January 14

This morning, enjoyed a most solemn season in prayer: my soul seemed enlarged, and assisted to pour out itself to God for grace, and for every blessing I wanted for myself, my dear Christian friends, and for the church of God; and was so enabled to see Him who is invisible, that my soul rested upon Him for the performance of everything I asked agreeable to His will. My soul confided in God for myself, and for His church; trusted in divine power and grace, that He would do glorious things in His church on earth, for His own glory.

January 23

I think I never felt more resigned to God, nor so dead to the world, in every respect, as now; am dead to all desire of reputation and greatness, either in life, or after death; all I long for, is to be holy, humble, and crucified to the world.

February 4

Enjoyed some degree of freedom and spiritual refreshment; was enabled to pray with some fervency, and with longing desires for the church's prosperity; and my faith and hope seemed to take hold of God, for the performance of what I was enabled to plead for. Sanctification in myself, and the ingathering of God's elect, were all my desire; and the hope of their accomplishment all my joy.

March 2

Was most of the day employed in writing on a divine subject. Was frequent in prayer, and enjoyed some small degree of assistance. But in the evening,

God was pleased to grant me divine sweetness in prayer; especially in the duty of intercession. I think, I never felt so much kindness and love to those who, I have reason to think, are my enemies,—though at that time I found such a disposition to think the best of all, that I scarce knew how to think that any such thing as enmity and hatred lodged in any soul; it seemed as if all the world must needs be friends. I never prayed with more freedom and delight for myself, or dearest friend, than I did now for my enemies.

March 3

In the morning, spent (I believe) an hour in prayer, with great intenseness and freedom, and with the most soft and tender affection towards mankind. I longed that those who, I have reason to think, bear me ill-will, might be eternally happy. It seemed refreshing to think of meeting them in heaven, how much soever they had injured me on earth. I had no disposition to insist upon any confession from them, in order to reconciliation and the exercise of love and kindness to them.

Oh, it is an emblem of heaven itself,

to love all the world with a love of kindness, forgiveness, and benevolence; to feel our souls sedate, mild and meek; to be void of all evil surmisings and suspicions, and scarce able to think evil of any man upon any occasion; to find our hearts simple, open, and free, to those that look upon us with a different eye!

Prayer was so sweet an exercise to me, that I knew not how to cease, lest I should lose the spirit of prayer. Felt no disposition to eat or drink, for the sake of the pleasure of it, but only to support my body, and fit me for divine service. Could not be content without a very particular mention of a great number of dear friends at the throne of grace; as also the particular circumstances of many, so far as they were known.

Lord's Day, March 4

In the morning, enjoyed the same intenseness in prayer as yesterday morning, though not in so great a degree: felt the same spirit of love, universal benevolence, forgiveness, humility, resignation, mortification to the world, and composure of mind, as then. My soul rested in God; and I found I wanted no other refuge or friend. While my soul thus trusts in God, all things seem to be at peace with me, even the stones of the earth: but when I cannot apprehend and confide in God, all things appear with a different aspect.

March 10

In the morning, felt exceeding dead to the world, and all its enjoyments. I thought I was ready and willing to give up life and all its comforts, as soon as called to it; and yet then had as much comfort of life as almost ever I had. Life itself now appeared but an empty bubble; the riches, honors, and common enjoyments of life appeared extremely tasteless.

I longed to be perpetually and entirely crucified to all things here below, by the cross of Christ. My soul was sweetly resigned to God's disposal of me, in every regard; and I saw that nothing had happened but what was best for me. I confided in God, that He would never leave me, though I should "walk through the valley of the shadow of death."

May 8

Set out from Sharon, in Connecticut, and traveled about forty-five miles to a place called Fishkill, and lodged there. Spent much of my time, while riding, in prayer, that God would go with me to Delaware. My heart, sometimes, was ready to sink with the thoughts of my work, and going alone in the wilderness, I knew not where; but still it was comfortable, to think, that others of God's children had "wandered about in caves and dens of the earth"; and Abraham, when he was called to go forth, "went out, not knowing whither he went." Oh, that I might follow after God!

June 27

Felt something of the same solemn concern, and spirit of prayer, which I enjoyed last night, soon after I rose in the morning. In the afternoon, rode several miles to see if I could procure any lands for the poor Indians, that they might live together, and be under advantages for instruction.

While I was riding, had a deep sense of the greatness and difficulty of my work; and my soul seemed to rely wholly upon God for success, in the diligent and faithful use of means. Saw, with the greatest certainty, that the arm of the Lord must be revealed, for the help of these poor heathen, if ever they were to be delivered from the bondage of the powers of darkness.

(See record of August 6, 1745, how at length the arm of the Lord was revealed indeed.)

3
The Long Night of Weeping

June 28, 1744

Spent the morning in reading several parts of the Holy Scripture, and in fervent prayer for my Indians, that God would set up His kingdom among them, and bring them into His church. About nine, I withdrew to my usual place of retirement in the woods; and there again enjoyed some assistance in prayer. My great concern was for the conversion of the heathen to God; and the Lord helped me to plead with Him for it.

Towards noon, rode up to the Indians, in order to preach to them; and, while going, my heart went up to God in prayer for them. Could freely tell God, He knew that the cause in which I was engaged was not mine; but that it was His own cause, and that it would be for His own glory to convert the poor Indians. And blessed be God, I felt no desire for their conversion, that I might receive honor from the world, as being the instrument of it. Had some freedom in speaking to the Indians.

July 6

Awoke this morning in the fear of God. After I arose, I spent some time in reading God's Word, and in prayer. I cried to God under a sense of my great indigence. Last year, I longed to be prepared for a world of glory, and speedily to depart out of this world; but of late all my concern, almost, is for the conversion of the heathen; and for that end I long to live. But blessed be God, I have less desire to live for any of the pleasures of the world, than I ever had.

I long and love to be a pilgrim; and want grace to imitate the life, labors, and sufferings of St. Paul among the heathen. And when I long for holiness now, it is not so much for myself as formerly; but rather that thereby I may become an "able minister of the New Covenant," especially to the heathen. Spent about two hours this morning in reading and prayer by turns; and was in a watchful, tender frame, afraid of everything that might cool my affections, and draw away my heart from God.

July 12

Towards night my burden respecting my work among the Indians began to increase much; and was aggravated by hearing sundry things, which looked very discouraging; in particular, that they intended to meet together the next day for an idolatrous feast and dance. Then I began to be in anguish. I thought that I must in conscience go and endeavor to break them up; yet knew not how to attempt such a thing. However, I withdrew for prayer, hoping for strength from above.

In prayer I was exceedingly enlarged, and my soul was as much drawn out as I ever remember it to have been in my life. I was in such anguish, and pleaded with so much earnestness and importunity, that when I rose from my knees I felt extremely weak and overcome; I could scarce walk straight; my joints were loosed; the sweat ran down my face and body; and nature seemed as if it would dissolve.

So far as I could judge, I was wholly free from selfish ends in my fervent supplications for the poor Indians. I knew that they were met together to worship devils, and not God: and this made me cry earnestly, that God would now appear, and help me in my attempts to break up this idolatrous meeting. My soul pleaded long; and I thought that God would hear, and would go with me to vindicate His own cause; I seemed to confide in God for His presence and assistance.

Thus I spent the evening, praying incessantly for divine assistance, and that I might not be self-dependent, but still have my whole dependence upon God. What I passed through was remarkable, and indeed inexpressible. All things here below vanished; and there appeared to be nothing of any considerable importance to me, but holiness of heart and life, and the conversion of the heathen to God.

All my cares, fears, and desires, which might be said to be of a worldly nature, disappeared; and were, in my esteem, of little more importance than a puff of wind. I exceedingly longed that God would get to Himself a name among the heathen; and I appealed to Him with the greatest freedom, that He knew I "preferred Him above my chief joy." Indeed, I had no notion of joy from this world; I cared not where or how I lived, or what hardships I went through, so that I could but gain souls to Christ.

I continued in this frame all the evening and night. While I was asleep, I dreamed all these things; and when I waked, the first thing I thought of was this great work of pleading for God against Satan.

Lord's Day, July 22

When I waked, my soul was burdened with what seemed to be before me. I cried to God, before I could get out of my bed; and as soon as I was dressed, I withdrew into the woods, to pour out my burdened soul to God, especially for assistance in my great work; for I could scarcely think of anything else. I enjoyed the same freedom and fervency as last evening; and did with unspeakable freedom give up myself afresh to God, for life or death, for all hardships He should call me to among the heathen; and felt as if nothing could discourage me from this blessed work. I had a strong hope that God would "bow the heavens and come down," and do some marvelous work among the heathen.

While I was riding to the Indians—three miles, my heart was continually going out to God for His presence and assistance; and hoping, and almost expecting, that God would make this the day of His power and grace among the poor Indians. When I came to them, I found them engaged in their frolic; but through divine goodness I persuaded them to desist, and attend to my preaching: yet still there appeared nothing of the special power of God among them.

Preached again to them in the afternoon, and observed the Indians were more sober than before; but still saw nothing special among them. Hence Satan took occasion to tempt and buffet me with these cursed suggestions: "There is no God, or if there be, He is not able to convert the Indians, before they have more knowledge," etc. I was very weak and weary, and my soul borne down with perplexity; but was mortified to all the world, and was determined still to wait upon God for the conversion of the heathen, though the devil tempted me to the contrary.

July 23

Retained still a deep and pressing sense of what lay with so much weight upon me yesterday; but was more calm and quiet. Enjoyed freedom and composure, after the temptations of last evening; had sweet resignation to the divine will; and desired nothing so much as the conversion of the heathen to God, and that His kingdom might come in my own heart, and the hearts of others.

July 24

Rode about seventeen miles westward, over a hideous mountain, to a number of Indians. Got together near thirty of them: preached to them in the evening, and lodged among them.

Was weak, and felt in some degree disconsolate; yet could have no freedom in the thought of any other circumstances or other business in life. All my desire was the conversion of the heathen; and all hope was in God. God does not suffer me to please or comfort myself with hopes of seeing friends, returning to my dear acquaintances, and enjoying worldly comforts.

Lord's Day, September 2

Was enabled to speak to my poor Indians with much concern and fervency; and I am persuaded that God enabled me to exercise faith in Him, while I was speaking to them. I perceived that some of them were afraid to hearken to and embrace Christianity, lest they should be enchanted and poisoned by some of the "powaws":

but I was enabled to plead with them not to fear these; and confiding in God for safety and deliverance—

I bid a challenge to all these powers of darkness, to do their worst on me first. I told my people that I was a Christian, and asked them why the "pow-aws" did not bewitch and poison me. I scarcely ever felt more sensible of my own unworthiness, than in this action. I saw that the honor of God was concerned in the affair; and I desired to be preserved—not from selfish views, but for a testimony of the divine power and goodness, and of the truth of Christianity, and that God might be glorified. Afterwards, I found my soul rejoice in God for His assisting grace.

October 8

Visited the Indians with a design to take my leave of them, supposing they would this morning go out to hunting early; but beyond my expectation and hope, they desired to hear me preach again. I gladly complied with their request, and afterwards endeavored to answer their objections against Christianity.

Then they went away; and we spent the rest of the afternoon in reading and prayer, intending to go homeward very early the next day. My soul was in some measure refreshed in secret prayer and meditation. Blessed be the Lord for all His goodness.

Lord's Day, October 14

Was much confused and perplexed in my thoughts; could not pray; and was almost discouraged, thinking I should never be able to preach any more. Afterwards, God was pleased to give me some relief from these confusions; but still I was afraid, and even troubled before God. I went to the place of public worship, lifting up my heart to God for assistance and grace, in my great work: and God was gracious to me, helping me to plead with Him for holiness, and to use the strongest arguments with Him, drawn from the incarnation and sufferings of Christ for this very end, that men might be made holy.

Afterwards, I was much assisted in preaching. I know not that ever God helped me to preach in a more close and distinguishing manner for the trial of men's state. Through the infinite goodness of God, I felt what I spoke; He enabled me to treat on divine truth with uncommon clearness; and yet I was so sensible of my defects in preaching, that I could not be proud of my performance, as at some times; and blessed be the Lord for this mercy!

In the evening I longed to be entirely alone, to bless God for help in a time of extremity; and longed for great degrees of holiness, that I might show my gratitude to God.

November 22

Came on my way from Rockciticus to the Delaware. Was very much disordered with a cold and pain in my head. About six at night, I lost my way in the wilderness, and wandered over rocks and mountains, down hideous steeps, through swamps, and most dreadful and dangerous places; and, the night being dark, so that few stars could be seen, I was greatly exposed. I was much pinched with cold, and distressed with an extreme pain in my head, attended with sickness at my stomach; so that every step I took was distressing to me.

I had little hope for several hours together, but that I must lie out in the woods all night, in this distressed case. But about nine o'clock I found a house, through the abundant goodness of God, and was kindly entertained. Thus I have frequently been exposed, and sometimes lain out the whole night: but God has hitherto preserved me; and blessed be His name. Such fatigues and hardships as these serve to wean me from the earth; and, I trust, will make heaven the sweeter.

January 3, 1745

Being sensible of a great want of divine influence, and the outpouring of God's Spirit, I spent this day in fasting and prayer, to seek so great a mercy for myself, my poor people in particular, and the church of God in general.

January 9

In the morning, God was pleased to remove that gloom which has of late oppressed my mind, and to give me freedom and sweetness in prayer. I was encouraged, strengthened, and enabled to plead for grace for myself, and mercy for my poor Indians; and was sweetly assisted in my intercessions with God for others.

Lord's Day, February 24

My discourse was suited to my own case, for of late I have found a great want of apprehension of divine grace and have often been greatly distressed in my soul, because I did not suitably apprehend this fountain opened to purge away sin; and so have been too much laboring for spiritual life, and peace of conscience, and progressive holiness in my own strength. But now God showed me in some measure the arm of all strength and the fountain of all grace.

(This is the secret of holiness that even earnest souls often miss. They magnify Law rather than Grace, they see the exceeding sinfulness of sin and forget the omnipotent Savior, deplore the guilt and stain, but do not extol the blood.)

4
The Joy of the Morning

(Having passed through the long night of weeping we now come as Jonathan Edwards reminds us to the joy of the morning. Prevailing prayer has at length brought down blessing, like Elijah's prayer for rain.)

Crossweeksung, June 19, 1745

I had spent most of my time, for more than a year past, among the Indians at the Forks of Delaware in Pennsylvania. During that time I made two journeys to the Susquehannah, to treat with the Indians on that river respecting Christianity; and, not having had any considerable appearance of special success in either of those places, my spirits were depressed, and I was not a little discouraged.

Hearing that there were a number of Indians at a place called Crossweeksung, in New Jersey, nearly eighty miles southeast from the Forks of Delaware, I determined to make them a visit, and see what might be done towards Christianizing them; and accordingly arrived among them on Wednesday, June 19th, 1745.

I found very few persons at the place which I visited, and perceived that the Indians in these parts were very much scattered. However, I preached to those few I found; who appeared well disposed, serious, and attentive, and not inclined to cavil and object, as the Indians had done elsewhere. When I had concluded my discourse, I informed them, there being none but a few women and children, that I would willingly visit them again the next day. Whereupon they readily set out and traveled ten or fifteen miles, in order to give notice to some of their friends at that distance.

June 20

Visited and preached to the Indians again as I proposed. Numbers were gathered at the invitations of their friends, who had heard me the day before. These also appeared as attentive, orderly, and well disposed as the others: and none made any objections, as Indians in other places have usually done. Towards night preached to the Indians again, and had more hearers than before.

June 22

About noon rode to the Indians again, and next night preached to them. Found my body much strengthened, and was enabled to speak with abundant plainness and warmth. Their number, which at first consisted of seven or eight persons, was now increased to nearly thirty. There was not only a solemn attention among them, but some considerable impression, it was apparent, was made upon their minds by divine truth. This was indeed a sweet afternoon to me. While riding, before I came to the Indians, my spirits were refreshed, and my soul was enabled to cry to God incessantly, for many miles together.

June 24

Preached to the Indians at their desire, and upon their own motion. To see poor pagans desirous of hearing the gospel of Christ, animated me to discourse to them; although I was now very weakly, and my spirits much exhausted.

June 27

Visited and preached to the Indians

again. Their number now amounted to about forty persons. Their solemnity and attention still continued, and a considerable concern for their souls became very apparent among numbers of them.

June 29

Preached twice to the Indians; and could not but wonder at their seriousness, and the strictness of their attention. Saw, as I thought, the hand of God very evidently, and in a manner somewhat remarkable, making provision for their subsistence together, in order to their being instructed in divine things. For this day, and the day before, with only walking a little way from the place of our daily meeting, they killed three deer, which were a seasonable supply for their wants, and without which, they could not have subsisted together in order to attend the means of grace.

5
Days of Blessing

(We now approach what Brainerd's biographer calls his "marvelous success"; but he reminds us that it is not in his public journal, but in his secret diary we find the sacred record of the intense travail and importunate prayers which preceded that miracle of grace; and to this must be added the conversion of his interpreter which took place at this time.

It appears that having left his Indians at Crossweeksung at the beginning of July, to visit others at the Forks of Delaware, he returned to them in August. The following extract shows the intense preparedness of his mind prior to the extraordinary awakening and Pentecostal outpouring.)

July 26, 1745
I longed that I might do something, if the Lord pleased, for His interest in the world. My soul, my very soul, longed for the ingathering of the poor heathen; and I cried to God most willingly and

heartily. I could not but cry. This was a sweet season; for I had some lively taste of heaven, and a temper of mind suited in some measure to the employments and entertainments of it. My soul was grieved to leave the place; but my body was weak and worn out, and it was nearly nine o'clock. I longed that the remaining part of life might be filled up with more fervency and activity in the things of God. Oh, the inward peace, composure, and godlike serenity of such a frame! Heaven must differ from this only in degree, not in kind. Lord! ever give me this Bread of Life.

Crossweeksung, August 2

In the evening, I retired, and my soul was drawn out in prayer to God; especially for my poor people, to whom I had sent word that they might gather together, that I might preach to them the next day. I was much enlarged in praying for their saving conversion; and scarcely ever found my desires for any thing of this nature so sensibly and clearly, to my own satisfaction, disinterested, and free from selfish views.

It seemed to me I had no care, or hardly any desire, to be the instrument of so glorious a work as I wished and prayed for among the Indians. If the blessed work might be accomplished to the honor of God, and the enlargement of the dear Redeemer's kingdom—this was all my desire and care; and for this mercy I hoped, but with trembling; for I felt what Job expresses, in 9:16, "If I had called, and He had answered me, yet would I not believe that He had hearkened unto my voice."

My rising hopes, respecting the conversion of the Indians, have been so often dashed, that my spirit is, as it were, broken, and my courage wasted and I hardly dare hope. I visited the Indians in these parts in June last, and tarried with them a considerable time, preaching almost daily; at which season God was pleased to pour upon them a spirit of awakening, and concern for their souls, and surprisingly to engage their attention to divine truths. I now found them serious, and a number of them under deep concern for an interest in Christ.

Their convictions of their sinful and perishing state were, in my absence from them, much promoted by the labors and endeavors of Rev. William Tennett; to whom I had advised them to apply for direction; and whose house they frequented much while I was gone. I preached to them this day with some view to Revelation 22:17: "And whosoever will, let him take the water of life freely." Though I could not pretend to handle the subject methodically among them, the Lord, I am persuaded, enabled me, in a manner somewhat uncommon, to set before them the Lord Jesus Christ as a kind and compassionate Savior, inviting distressed and perishing sinners to accept everlasting mercy.

A surprising concern soon became apparent among them. There were only about twenty adult persons together; many of the Indians, at remote places, not having, as yet, had time to come since my return hither. Not above two that I could see had dry eyes. Some were much concerned, and discovered vehement longings of soul after Christ, to save them from the misery they felt and feared.

Lord's Day, August 4

Being invited by a neighboring minister to assist in the administration of the Lord's supper, I complied with his request, and took the Indians along with me; not only those who were together the day before, but many more who were coming to hear me; so that there were nearly fifty in all, old and young. They attended the several discourses of the day; and some of them, who could understand English, were much affected; and all seemed to have their concern in some measure raised.

Now a change in their manners began to appear very visible. In the evening, when they came to sup together, they would not take a morsel until they had sent to me to come and supplicate a blessing on their food; at which time sundry of them wept; especially when I reminded them they had, in times past, eaten their feasts in honor of devils, and neglected to thank God for His gifts.

August 5

After a sermon had been preached by another minister, I preached, and concluded the public work of the solemnity from John 7:37: "In the last day," etc.; and, in my discourse, addressed the Indians in particular, who sat in a part of the house by themselves; at which time, their concern increased to a considerable degree.

In the evening, the greater part of

them being at the house where I lodged, I discoursed to them; and found them universally engaged about their souls' concerns; inquiring "what they should do to be saved." All their conversation among themselves turned upon religious matters, in which they were much assisted by my interpreter, who was with them day and night.

This day one woman, who had been much concerned for her soul ever since she first heard me preach in June last, obtained comfort, I trust, solid and well-grounded. She seemed to be filled with love to Christ. At the same time she behaved humbly and tenderly, and appeared afraid of nothing so much as of offending and grieving Him whom her soul loved.

August 6

In the morning I discoursed to the Indians at the house where we lodged. Many of them were much affected, and appeared surprisingly tender; so that a few words about the concerns of their souls would cause the tears to flow freely, and produce many sobs.

In the afternoon, they being returned to the place where I had usually preached among them, I again discoursed to them there. There were about fifty-five that were capable of attending divine service with understanding. I insisted on I John 4:10, "Herein is love," etc. They seemed eager of hearing; but there appeared nothing very remarkable, except their attention, till near the close of my discourse; and then divine truths were attended with a surprising influence, and produced a great concern among them.

There were scarcely three in forty who could refrain from tears and bitter cries. They all as one seemed in an agony of soul to obtain an interest in Christ; and the more I discoursed of the love and compassion of God in sending His Son to suffer for the sins of men, and the more I invited them to come and partake of His love, the more their distress was aggravated, because they felt themselves unable to come. It was surprising to see how their hearts seemed to be pierced with the tender and melting invitations of the gospel, when there was not a word of terror spoken to them.

There were this day two persons who obtained relief and comfort; which, when I came to discourse with them particularly, appeared solid, rational, and Scriptural. After I had inquired into the grounds of their comfort, and said many things which I thought proper to them, I asked them what they wanted that God should do further for them. They replied, "that they wanted Christ should wipe their hearts quite clean," etc. So surprising were now the doings of the Lord, that I can say no less of this day, and I need say no more of it, than that the arm of the Lord was powerfully and marvelously revealed in it.

August 7

Preached to the Indians from Isaiah 53:3–10. There was a remarkable influence attending the Word, and great concern in the assembly; but scarcely equal to what appeared the day before; that is, not quite so universal. However, most were much affected, and many in great distress for their souls; and some few could neither go nor stand, but lay flat on the ground, as if pierced at heart, crying incessantly for mercy. Several were newly awakened; and it was remarkable that, as fast as they came from remote places round about, the

Spirit of God seemed to seize them with concern for their souls.

After public service was concluded, I found two persons more who had newly met with comfort, of whom I had good hopes; and a third, of whom I could not but entertain some hopes, whose case did not appear as clear as the others; so that there were now six in all who had got some relief from their spiritual distresses; and five, whose experience appeared very clear and satisfactory. It is worthy of remark, that those who obtained comfort first, were in general deeply affected with concern for their souls when I preached to them in June last.

August 8

In the afternoon I preached to the Indians, their number was now about sixty-five persons—men, women and children. I discoursed upon Luke 14:16–23, and was favored with uncommon freedom in my discourse. There was much visible concern among them, while I was discoursing publicly; but afterwards, when I spoke to one and another more particularly, whom I perceived under much concern, the power of God seemed to descend upon the assembly "like a mighty rushing wind," and with an astonishing energy bore down all before it.

I stood amazed at the influence, which seized the audience almost universally; and could compare it to nothing more aptly, than the irresistible force of a mighty torrent, or a swelling deluge, that with its insupportable weight and pressure bears down and sweeps before it whatever comes in its way. Almost all persons of all ages were bowed down with concern together, and scarcely one was able to withstand the shock of this surprising operation.

Old men and women, who had been drunken wretches for many years, and some little children, not more than six or seven years of age, appeared in distress for their souls, as well as persons of middle age. It was apparent that these children, some of them at least, were not merely frightened with seeing the general concern; but were made sensible of their danger, the badness of their hearts, and their misery without Christ, as some of them express it. The most stubborn hearts were now obliged to bow.

A principal man among the Indians, who before was most secure and self-righteous, and thought his state good, because he knew more than the generality of the Indians had formerly done, and who with a great degree of confidence the day before told me "he had been a Christian more than ten years," was now brought under solemn concern for his soul, and wept bitterly.

Another man advanced in years, who had been a murderer, a "powaw," or conjurer, and a notorious drunkard, was likewise brought now to cry for mercy with many tears, and to complain much that he could be no more concerned when he saw his danger so very great.

There was almost universal praying and crying for mercy in every part of the house, and many out of doors; and numbers could neither go nor stand. Their concern was so great, each one for himself, that none seemed to take any notice of those about him, but each prayed freely for himself. I am led to think they were, to their own apprehensions, as much retired as if they had been, individually by themselves, in the thickest desert; or I believe rather that they thought nothing about anything but themselves, and their own state, and so were every one praying apart, although all together.

It seemed to me that there was now an exact fulfilment of that prophecy (Zech. 12:10, 11, 12); for there was now "a great mourning, like the mourning of Hadadrimmon"; and each seemed to "mourn apart." I thought this had a near resemblance to that day of God's power, mentioned in Joshua 10:14; for I must say I never saw any day like it, in all respects: it was a day wherein I am persuaded the Lord did much to destroy the kingdom of darkness among this people.

The concern, in general, was most rational and just. Those who had been awakened any considerable time, complained more especially of the badness of their hearts; and those who were newly awakened, of the badness of their lives and actions; and all were afraid of the anger of God, and of everlasting misery as the desert of their sins.

Some of the white people, who came out of curiosity to hear what "this babbler would say" to the poor ignorant Indians, were much awakened; and some appeared to be wounded with a view of their perishing state. Those who had lately obtained relief, were filled with comfort at this season. They appeared calm and composed, and seemed to rejoice in Christ Jesus.

Some of them took their distressed friends by the hand, telling them of the goodness of Christ, and the comfort that is to be enjoyed in Him; and thence invited them to come and give up their hearts to Him. I could observe some of them, in the most honest and unaffected manner, without any design of being taken notice of, lifting up their eyes to heaven, as if crying for mercy, while they saw the distress of the poor souls around them.

There was one quite remarkable instance of awakening this day which I cannot fail to notice here. A young Indian woman, who, I believe, never knew before that she had a soul, nor ever thought of any such thing, hearing that there was something strange among the Indians, came, it seems, to see what was the matter. On her way to the Indians she called at my lodgings; and when I told her that I designed presently to preach to the Indians, she laughed, and seemed to mock; but went however to them.

I had not proceeded far in my public discourse before she felt effectually that she had a soul; and, before I had concluded my discourse, was so convinced of her sin and misery, and so distressed with concern for her soul's salvation, that she seemed like one pierced through with a dart, and she cried out incessantly. She could neither go nor stand, nor sit on her seat without being held up.

After public service was over, she lay flat on the ground, praying earnestly, and would take no notice of, nor give any answer to, any who spoke to her. I hearkened to hear what she said, and perceived the burden of her prayer to be: *"Guttummaukalummeh wechaumeh kmeleh Nolah"*; i.e., *"Have mercy on me, and help me give You my heart."* Thus she continued praying incessantly for hours together.

This was indeed a surprising day of God's power, and seemed enough to convince an atheist of the truth, importance, and power of God's Word.

August 9

Spent almost the whole day with the Indians; the former part of it in discoursing to many of them privately. In the afternoon discoursed to them publicly. There were now present about seventy persons, old and young. I opened and applied the Parable of the Sower, Matthew 13. Was enabled to discourse with much plainness, and found afterwards that this discourse was very instructive to them.

There were many tears among them, while I was discoursing publicly, but no considerable cry; yet some were much affected with a few words spoken from Matthew 11:28: "Come unto Me, all ye that labor," with which I concluded my discourse. But, while I was discoursing near night to two or three of the awakened persons, a divine influence seemed to attend what was spoken to them in a powerful manner; which caused the persons to cry out in anguish of soul, although I spoke not a word of terror, but on the contrary, set before them the fullness and all-sufficiency of Christ's merits, and His willingness to save all that come to Him, and thereupon pressed them to come without delay.

The cry of these was soon heard by others, who, though scattered before, immediately gathered round. I then proceeded in the same strain of gospel invitation, till they were all melted into tears and cries, except two or three; and seemed in the greatest distress to find and secure an interest in the great Redeemer.

Some, who had little more than a ruffle made in their passions the day before, seemed now to be deeply affected and wounded at heart; and the concern in general appeared nearly as prevalent as it was the day before. There was indeed a very great mourning among them, and yet every one seemed to mourn apart. For so great was their concern, that almost every one was praying and crying for himself, as if none had been near. *"Guttummaukalummeh; guttummaukalummeh,"*—*"Have mercy upon me; have mercy upon me,"* was the common cry.

It was very affecting to see the poor Indians, who the other day were hallooing and yelling in their idolatrous feasts and drunken frolics, now crying to God with such importunity for an interest in His dear Son! Found two or three persons who, I had reason to hope, had taken comfort upon good grounds since the evening before; and these, with others who had obtained comfort, were together, and seemed to rejoice much that God was carrying on His work with such power upon others.

August 24

Spent the forenoon in discoursing to some of the Indians, in order to their receiving the ordinance of baptism. When I had opened the nature of the ordinance, the obligations attending it, the duty of devoting ourselves to God in it, and the privilege of being in covenant with Him; numbers of them seemed to be filled with love to God, delighted with the thoughts of giving themselves up to Him in that solemn and public manner, and melted and refreshed with the hopes of enjoying the blessed Redeemer.

The reader's attention is called to that primitive and Pentecostal nature of their open profession of Christianity in baptism, by calculating the shortness of the interval elapsing between their first hearing the gospel, and their great readiness for making public acknowledgment of their faith.

There were several Indians newly come, who thought their state good, and themselves happy, because they had sometimes lived with the white people under gospel light, had learned to read, were civil, etc., although they appeared utter strangers to their own hearts, and altogether unacquainted with the power of religion, as well as with the doctrines of grace.

With these I discoursed particularly after public worship; and was surprised to see their self-righteous dispositions, their strong attachment to the covenant of works for salvation, and the high value they put upon their supposed attainments. Yet, after much discourse, one appeared in a measure convinced that "by the deeds of the law no flesh living can be justified"; and wept bitterly, inquiring what he must do to be saved.

Lord's Day, August 25

After the crowd of spectators was gone, I called the baptized persons together, and discoursed to them in particular; at the same time inviting others to attend. I reminded them of the solemn obligations they were now under to live to God; warned them of the evil and dreadful consequences of careless living, especially after their public profession of Christianity; gave them directions for future conduct; and encouraged them to watchfulness and devotion, by setting before them the comfort and happy conclusion of a religious life.

This was a desirable and sweet season indeed! Their hearts were engaged and cheerful in duty; and they rejoiced that they had, in a public and solemn manner, dedicated themselves to God. Love seemed to reign among them! They took each other by the hand with tenderness and affection, as if their hearts were knit together, while I was discoursing to them; and all their deportment towards each other was such, that a serious spectator might justly be excited to cry out with admiration: "Behold how they love one another!"

Numbers of the other Indians, on seeing and hearing these things, were much affected, and wept bitterly; longing to be partakers of the same joy and comfort, which these discovered by their very countenances, as well as by their conduct. I rode to my lodgings in the evening, blessing the Lord for His gracious visitation of the Indians, and the soul-refreshing things I had seen the days past among them; and praying that God would still carry on His divine work among them.

6
Sunshine and Shadow

BEING NOW CONVINCED that it was my duty to take a journey far back to the Indians on the Susquehannah, it being now a proper season of the year to find them generally at home; after having spent some hours in public and private discourse with my people, I told them that I must now leave them for the present, and go to their brethren far remote, and preach to them; that I wanted the Spirit of God should go with me, without whom nothing could be done to any good purpose among the Indians—as they themselves had opportunity to see and observe by the barrenness of our meetings at sometimes, when there was much pains taken to affect and awaken sinners, and yet to little or no purpose.

I asked them if they would not be willing to spend the remainder of the day in prayer for me, that God would go with me, and prosper my endeavors for the conversion of these poor souls. They cheerfully complied with the motion, and soon after I left them, the sun being about an hour and a half high at night, they began, and they continued praying till break of day, or very near: never thinking, as they tell me, till they went out and viewed the stars, and saw the morning star a considerable height, that it was later than bed time. Thus eager and unwearied were they in their devotions!

A remarkable night it was; attended, as my interpreter tells me, with a powerful influence upon those who were yet under concern, as well as those who had received comfort. There were, I trust, this day, two distressed souls brought to the enjoyment of solid comfort in Him in whom the weary find rest.

It was likewise remarkable, that this day an old Indian, who had all his days been an idolater, was brought to give up his rattles, which they used for music in their idolatrous feasts and dances, to the other Indians, who quickly destroyed them. This was done without any attempt of mine in the affair, I having said nothing to him about it, so that it seemed to be nothing but the power of God's Word, without any particular application to this sin, that produced this effect. Thus God has begun; thus He has hitherto surprisingly carried on a work of grace amongst these Indians. May the glory be ascribed to Him who is the sole Author of it!

I went from the Indians to my lodgings, rejoicing for the goodness of God to my poor people; and enjoyed freedom of soul in prayer, and other duties, in the evening. Bless the Lord, O my soul!

Forks of Delaware, Pennsylvania,
Lord's Day, September 1

Preached to the Indians from Luke 11:16–23. The word appeared to be attended with some power, and caused some tears in the assembly. Afterwards preached to a number of white people present, and observed many of them in tears; and some who had formerly been as careless and unconcerned about religion, perhaps, as the Indians. Toward night, discoursed to the Indians again, and perceived a greater attention, and more visible concern among them, than has been usual in these parts. God gave me the spirit of prayer, and it was a blessed season in that respect.

September 5

Discoursed to the Indians from the

parable of the sower. Afterwards I conversed particularly with sundry persons; which occasioned them to weep, and even to cry out in an affecting manner; which caused others to be seized with surprise and concern. I doubt not but that a divine power accompanied what was then spoken.

Several of these persons had been with me to Crossweeksung; and there had seen, and some of them, I trust, felt, the power of God's Word, in an affecting and saving manner. I asked one of them, who had obtained comfort and given hopeful evidences of being truly religious, why he now cried. He replied: "When he thought how Christ was slain like a lamb, and spilt His blood for sinners, he could not help crying, when he was alone"; and thereupon burst into tears, and cried again.

I then asked his wife, who had likewise been abundantly comforted, why she cried. She answered that she was grieved that the Indians here would not come to Christ, as well as those at Crossweeksung. I asked her if she found a heart to pray for them; and whether Christ had seemed to be near her of late in prayer, as in times past: which is my usual method of expressing a sense of the divine presence. She replied, Yes, He had been near her, and at times when she had been praying alone, her heart loved to pray so that she could not bear to leave the place, but wanted to stay and pray longer.

Lord's Day, September 8

Discoursed to the Indians in the afternoon from Acts 2:36–39. The Word of God at this time seemed to fall with weight and influence upon them. There were but few present; but most that were, were in tears; and several cried out in distressing concern for their souls. There was one man considerably awakened, who never before discovered any concern for his soul.

There appeared a remarkable work of the divine Spirit among them generally, not unlike what has been of late at Crossweeksung. It seemed as if the divine influence had spread thence to this place; although something of it appeared here before in the awakening of my interpreter, his wife, and some few others. Several of the careless white people now present were awakened, or at least startled, at seeing the power of God so prevalent among the Indians. I then made a particular address to them, which seemed to make some impression upon them, and excite some affection in them.

There are sundry Indians in these parts who have always refused to hear me preach, and have been enraged against those who have attended on my preaching. But of late they are more bitter than ever, scoffing at Christianity, and sometimes asking my hearers how often they have cried and whether they have not now cried enough to do their turn. The Christians are already having trial of cruel mockings.

In the evening, God was pleased to assist me in prayer, and give me freedom at the throne of grace. My soul was so engaged and enlarged in the sweet exercise, that I spent an hour in it, and knew not how to leave the mercy seat. Oh, how I delighted to pray and cry to God! I saw that God was both able and willing to do all that I desired for myself, and His church in general. I was likewise much enlarged and assisted in family prayer. Afterwards, when I was just going to bed, God helped me to renew my petition, with ardor and freedom. Oh, it was to me a blessed evening of prayer! Bless the Lord, O my soul!

September 9

Left the Indians at the Forks of Delaware, and set out on a journey toward Susquehannah River; directing my course towards an Indian town more than a hundred and twenty miles westward from the Forks.

Shaumoking, September 13

After having lodged out three nights, arrived at the Indian town I aimed at on the Susquehannah, called *Shaumoking*; one of the places (and the largest of them) which I visited in May last. I was kindly received, and entertained by the Indians; but had little satisfaction, by reason of the heathenish dance and revel they then held in the house where I was obliged to lodge; which I could not suppress, though I often entreated them to desist, for the sake of one of their own friends who was then sick in the house, and whose disorder was much aggravated by the noise.

Alas! How destitute of natural affection are these poor uncultivated pagans! Though they seemed somewhat kind in their own way. Of a truth the dark places of the earth are full of the habitations of cruelty. The Indians of this place are accounted the most drunken, mischievous, and ruffianlike fellows, of any in these parts; and Satan seems to have his seat in this town in an eminent manner.

September 20

Visited Indians again, and found them almost universally very busy in making preparations for a great sacrifice and dance. In the evening they met together, nearly a hundred of them, and danced around a large fire, having prepared ten fat deer for the sacrifice. The fat of the innards they burnt in the fire while they were dancing, and sometimes raised the flame to a prodigious height; at the same time yelling and shouting in such a manner, that they might easily have been heard two miles or more. They continued their sacred dance nearly all night, after which they ate the flesh of the sacrifice, and so retired each one to his own lodging.

I enjoyed little satisfaction, being entirely alone on the island as to any Christian company, and in the midst of this idolatrous revel; and having walked to and fro till body and mind were pained and much oppressed, I at length crept into a little crib made for corn, and there slept on the poles.

(After this ineffectual attempt he returned to Crossweeksung.)

7
Converts Growing in Grace

October 5, 1745
Preached to my people from John 14:1-6. The divine presence seemed to be in the assembly. Numbers were affected with divine truths, and it was a comfort to some in particular. Oh, what a difference is there between these, and the Indians with whom I have lately treated upon the Susquehannah!

To be with those seemed to be like being banished from God and all His people; to be with these, like being admitted into His family, and to the enjoyment of His divine presence! How great is the change lately made upon numbers of these Indians, who, not many months ago, were as thoughtless and averse to Christianity as those upon the Susquehannah! And how astonishing is that grace, which has made this change!

Lord's Day, October 6
Preached in the forenoon from John 10:7-11. There was a considerable melting among my people; the dear

young Christians were refreshed, comforted and strengthened; and one or two persons newly awakened. In the afternoon I discoursed on the story of the jailer, Acts 16; and in the evening, expounded Acts 20:1-12. There was at this time a very agreeable melting spread throughout the whole assembly. I think I scarce ever saw a more desirable affection in any number of people in my life. There was scarcely a dry eye to be seen among them; and yet nothing boisterous or unseemly, nothing that tended to disturb the public worship; but rather to encourage and excite a Christian ardor and spirit of devotion.

After public service was over, I withdrew, being much tired with the labors of the day; and the Indians continued praying among themselves for nearly two hours together; which continued exercises appeared to be attended with a blessed quickening influence from on high. I could not but earnestly wish that numbers of God's people had been present at this season to see and hear these things, which I am sure must refresh the heart of every true lover of the church's interests.

To see those who were very lately

savage pagans and idolaters, having no hope, and without God in the world, now filled with a sense of divine love and grace, and worshiping the Father in spirit and in truth, as numbers have appeared to do, was not a little affecting; and especially to see them appear so tender and humble, as well as lively, fervent, and devout in the divine service.

October 24

Discoursed from John 4:13, 14. There was a great attention, a desirable affection, and an unaffected melting in the assembly. It is surprising to see how eager they are to hear the Word of God. I have oftentimes thought that they would cheerfully and diligently attend divine worship twenty-four hours together if they had an opportunity so to do.

October 28

Discoursed from Matthew 22:1-13. I was enabled to open the Scriptures, and adapt my discourse and expression to the capacities of my people, I know not how, in a plain, easy, and familiar manner, beyond all I could have done by the utmost study: and this without any special difficulty; yea, with as much freedom as if I had been addressing an audience of people who had been instructed in the doctrines of Christianity all their days.

The Word of God, at this time, seemed to fall upon the assembly with a divine power and influence, especially towards the close of my discourse. There was both a sweet melting and bitter mourning in the audience. The dear Christians were refreshed and comforted, convictions revived in others, and several persons newly awakened, who had never been with us before. So much of the divine presence appeared in the assembly, that it seemed "this was no other than the house of God and the gate of Heaven."

All who had any savor and relish of divine things were constrained by the sweetness of that season to say: "Lord, it is good for us to be here." If ever there was among my people an appearance of the New Jerusalem "as a bride adorned for her husband," there was much of it at this time, and so agreeable was the entertainment, where such tokens of the divine presence were, that I could scarcely be willing in the evening to leave, and repair to my lodgings.

I was refreshed with a view of the continuance of this blessed work among them, and with its influence upon the strangers among the Indians, who had of late, from time to time, providentially come into this part of the country. Had an evening of sweet refreshing; my thoughts were raised to a blessed eternity; my soul was melted with desires of perfect holiness, and of perfectly glorifying God.

Lord's Day, November 3

I baptized fourteen persons of the Indians. One of these was nearly fourscore years of age; and I have reason to hope, that God had brought her savingly home to Himself. Two of the others were men of fifty years old, who had been singular and remarkable among the Indians for their wickedness. One of them had been a murderer, and both notorious drunkards, as well as excessively quarrelsome; but now I cannot but hope, that both of them have become subjects of God's special grace, especially the worst of the two.

November 4

Discoursed from John 11, briefly explaining most of the chapter. Divine truths made deep impressions upon many in the assembly. Numbers were affected with a view of the power of Christ, manifested in His raising the dead.

There were numbers of those who had come here lately from remote places, who were now brought under deep and pressing concern for their souls. One in particular, who, not long since, came half-drunk, and railed on us, and attempted by all means to disturb us while engaged in divine worship, was now so concerned and distressed for her soul, that she seemed unable to get any ease without an interest in Christ. There were many tears and affectionate sobs and groans in the assembly in general; some weeping for themselves, others for their friends.

Although persons are, doubtless, much more easily affected now than they were in the beginning of this religious concern, when tears and cries for their souls were things unheard of among them, yet I must say, that their affection in general appeared genuine and unfeigned; and, especially, this appeared very conspicuous in those newly awakened. So that true and genuine convictions of sin seem still to be begun and promoted in many instances.

8
The Gracious Ways of the Lord

IT IS REMARKABLE, that God began this work among the Indians at a time when I had the least hope, and, to my apprehension, the least rational prospect, of seeing a work of grace propagated among them: my bodily strength being then much wasted by a late tedious journey to the Susquehannah, where I was necessarily exposed to hardships and fatigues among the Indians; my mind being, also, exceedingly depressed with a view of the unsuccessfulness of my labors. I had little reason so much as to hope, that God had made me instrumental in the saving conversion of any of the Indians, except my interpreter and his wife. Hence I was ready to look upon myself as a burden to the honorable society which employed and supported me in this business, and began to entertain serious thoughts of giving up my mission.

My hopes respecting the conversion of the Indians were perhaps never reduced to so low an ebb, since I had any special concern for them, as at this time. Yet this was the very season in which God saw fit to begin this glorious work! Thus He "ordained strength out of weakness," by making bare His almighty arm, at a time when all hopes and human probabilities most evidently appeared to fail. Whence I learn, that it is good to follow the path of duty, though in the midst of darkness and discouragement.

My interpreter had before gained some good degree of doctrinal knowledge, whereby he was rendered capable of understanding, and communicating without mistakes, the intent and meaning of my discourses, and that without being confined strictly and obliged to interpret verbatim. He had likewise, to appearance, an experimental acquaintance with divine things; and it pleased God at this season to inspire his mind with longing desires for the conversion of the Indians, and to give him admirable zeal and fervency in addressing them in order thereto.

It is remarkable, that, when I was favored with any special assistance in any work, and enabled to speak with more than common freedom, fervency, and power, under a lively and affecting sense of divine things, he was usually affected in the same manner almost instantly, and seemed at once quickened and enabled to speak in the same pathetic language, and under the same influence that I did.

A surprising energy often accompanied the word at such seasons; so that the face of the whole assembly would be apparently changed almost in an instant, and tears and sobs became common among them.

But still, this great awakening, this surprising concern, was never excited by any harangues of terror, but always appeared most remarkable when I insisted upon the compassion of a dying Savior, the plentiful provisions of the gospel, and the free offers of divine grace to needy, distressed sinners.

The effects of this work have been very remarkable. I doubt not but that many of these people have gained more doctrinal knowledge of divine truths since I have first visited them in June last than could have been instilled into their minds by the most diligent use of proper and instructive means for whole years together, without such a divine influence. Their pagan notions and idolatrous practices seem to be entirely abandoned in these parts.

They seem generally divorced from drunkenness, their darling vice, the "sin that easily besets them"; so that I do not know of more than two that have been my steady hearers, who have drunk to excess since I first visited them; although, before, it was common for some or other of them to be drunk almost every day: and some of them seem now to fear this sin in particular more than death itself.

A principle of honesty and justice appears in many of them; and they seem concerned to discharge their old debts, which they have neglected, and perhaps scarcely thought of for years past. Love seems to reign among them, especially those who have given evidences of having passed a saving change: and I never saw any appearance of bitterness or censoriousness in these, nor any disposition to "esteem themselves better than others."

As their sorrows under convictions have been great and pressing, so many of them have since appeared to "rejoice with joy unspeakable, and full of glory''; and yet I never saw any thing ecstatic or flighty in their joy. Their consolations do not incline them to lightness; but, on the contrary, are attended with solemnity, and oftentimes with tears, and an apparent brokenness of heart. In this respect, some of them have been surprised at themselves, and have with concern observed to me, that when their hearts have been glad (which is a phrase they commonly make use of to express spiritual joy), they could not help crying.

June 19, 1746

This day makes up a complete year from the first time of my preaching to these Indians in New Jersey. What amazing things has God wrought in this space of time, for this poor people! What a surprising change appears in their tempers and behavior! How are morose and savage pagans, in this short period, transformed into agreeable, affectionate, and humble Christians, and their drunken and pagan howlings turned into devout and fervent praises to God! They ''who were sometimes darkness are now become light in the Lord.'' May they ''walk as children of the light and of the day!" And now to Him that is of power to establish them according to the gospel, and the preaching of Christ—to God only wise, be glory through Jesus Christ, for ever and ever, Amen.

9
Worn-out but Triumphant

(After this grateful humble review of what God had wrought through him, we read of Brainerd's increasing weakness, and the alarming symptoms which presaged his approaching dissolution. His public journal records many journeys in the prosecution of his persistent efforts to Christianize the heathen. We read that he visited the Delaware Indians, and preached to their king.

On several occasions he assisted some godly pastors in their services to the white communities. Oftentimes, however, he had to decline through excessive weakness. Once this weakness was so great that he almost fell off his horse when riding through the woods. It became painfully evident that he had the sentence of death in himself, brought on like the illness of Epaphroditus, through exposure to the hardships of his wilderness life.

A searching question may be asked, whether the Society who employed him was altogether guiltless in not providing more carefully for his comfort; and a sad reflection may be offered, that though in death the church has greatly honored him yet in life he was so neglected!

He has at length to say farewell to his beloved flock, a real church in the wilderness, then to journey to the home of Jonathan Edwards, where, in the presence of those who nursed his declining body, his seraphic spirit passed triumphantly into the presence of One who was the chiefest among ten thousand and the altogether lovely.)

November 3, 1746

Being now in so weak and low a state, that I was utterly incapable of performing my work, and having little hope of recovery, unless by much riding, I thought it my duty to take a long journey into New England, and to divert myself among my friends, whom I had not now seen for a long time. Accordingly I took leave of my congregation this day.

Before I left my people, I visited them all in their respective houses, and discoursed to each one, as I thought most proper and suitable for their circumstances, and found great freedom and assistance in so doing. I scarcely left one house but some were in tears; and many were not only affected with my being about to leave them, but with the solemn addresses I made them upon divine things; for I was helped to be fervent in spirit, while I discoursed to them.

(He was not able to visit his beloved Indians again. He traveled, by slow stages, on to New England, arriving at the home of Jonathan Edwards in the spring, where he died in the autumn of the same year, 1747. The following letter was written shortly before his lamented death to the Rev. John Brainerd, his brother, then laboring among the Indians of New Jersey.)

Dear Brother:
I am now just on the verge of Eternity, expecting very speedily to appear in an unseen world. I feel myself no more an inhabitant of earth, and sometimes earnestly long to "depart and be with Christ." I bless God; He has for some years given me an abiding conviction that it is impossible for any

rational creature to enjoy true happiness, without being entirely devoted to Him. Under the influence of this conviction I have in some measure acted. Oh, that I had done so more!

I saw both the excellency and necessity of holiness in life; but never in such a manner as now, when I am just brought from the sides of the grave. Oh, my brother, pursue after personal holiness; press towards that blessed mark. Be as much in fasting and prayer as your health will allow, and live above the rate of common Christians.

Charge my people in the name of their dying minister, yea, in the name of Him who was dead and is alive, to live and walk as becomes the gospel. Tell them how great the expectations of God and His people are from them, and how awfully they will wound God's cause, if they fall into vice; as well as fatally prejudice other poor Indians. Always insist that their experiences are rotten, that their joys are delusive, although they may have been rapt up into the third heaven in their own conceit by them, unless the main tenor of their lives be spiritual, watchful, and holy. In pressing these things, "thou shalt both save thyself and those that hear thee.''

God knows I was heartily willing to have served Him longer in the work of the ministry, although it had still been attended with all the labors and hardships of past years, if He had seen fit that it should be so: but as His will now appears otherwise, I am fully content, and can with the utmost freedom say: ''The will of the lord be done.''

Your affectionate dying brother,

DAVID BRAINERD

Mr. Edwards, among other things, relates the following of the days preceding Brainerd's death:

"The extraordinary frame he was in, on the evening of September 19, could not be hid. His mouth spake out of the abundance of his heart, expressing in a very affecting manner much the same things as are written in his diary. Among very many other extraordinary expressions, which he then uttered, were such as these: 'My heaven is to please God, and glorify Him, and to give all to Him, and to be wholly devoted to His glory: that is the heaven I long for; that is my religion, and that is my happiness, and always was ever since I suppose I had any true religion; and all those that are of that religion shall meet me in heaven.

" 'I do not go to heaven to be advanced, but to give honor to God. It is no matter where I shall be stationed in heaven, whether I have a high or a low seat there; but to love, and please, and glorify God is all. Had I a thousand souls, if they were worth anything, I would give them all to God; but I have nothing to give, when all is done.'

"Again, on September 27: 'Oh, why is His chariot so long in coming? Why tarry the wheels of His chariot? I am very willing to part with all; I am very willing to part with my dear brother John, and never see him again, to go to be for ever with the Lord. Oh, when I go there, how will God's dear church on earth be upon my mind!'

"Afterwards, the same morning, being asked how he did, he answered: 'I am almost in eternity. I long to be there. My work is done; I have done with all my friends; all the world is nothing to me. I long to be in heaven, praising and glorifying God with the holy angels. All my desire is to glorify God.'

"He said to me, one morning, as I came into his room: 'My thoughts have been employed on the old dear theme, the prosperity of God's church on earth. As I waked out of sleep, I was led to cry for the pouring out of God's Spirit, and the advancement of Christ's kingdom, for which the Redeemer did and suffered so much. It is that especially which makes me long for it.'

"He also dwelt much on the great importance of the work of gospel ministers, and expressed his longings, that they might be filled with the Spirit of God. He manifested much desire to see some of the neighboring ministers, with whom he had some acquaintance, and of whose sincere friendship he was confident, that he might converse freely with them on that subject, before he died. And it so happened that he had opportunity with some of them according to his desire.

"Another thing that lay much on his heart, from time to time, in these near approaches of death, was the spiritual prosperity of his own congregation of Christian Indians in New Jersey; and when he spake of them, it was with peculiar tenderness; so that his speech would be presently interrupted and drowned with tears."

This passage closed Brainerd's Diary, and was written just a week before his death:

October 2, 1747

My soul was this day, at turns, sweetly set on God; I longed to be with Him, that I might behold His glory. I felt sweetly disposed to commit all to Him, even my dearest friends, my dearest flock, my absent brother, and all my concerns for time and eternity. Oh, that His kingdom might come in the world; that they might all love and glorify Him, for what he is in Himself; and that the blessed Redeemer might see of the travail of His soul, and be satisfied! O come, Lord Jesus. Come quickly! Amen.

Let us, as we watch his heavenward translation, pray like Elisha. Oh, that we might receive a double portion of his spirit—his love for the heathen and his longing that the kingdom of Christ might speedily come.